CAREERS WITH

MUSEUMS

IF YOU LIKE TO SPEND YOUR DAYS AT the museum, there is a wide variety of interesting jobs that make working at these repositories of historical and significant artifacts, artwork, and data, a fascinating career choice.

People are mesmerized by museums and the behind-the-scenes work that makes these venues time capsules for the treasures of past generations. Museums are where history comes alive, visitors venture into a bygone era, and they have a chance to see the relics they have only read about in books. Rare art, noteworthy documents that hold a prominent place in history, tools used in the stone age, costumes worn in celebrated movies, weapons and uniforms from the American Revolutionary War, the laboratory instruments used to make an important scientific discovery, and so much more can be found in the thousands of museums across the United States.

Not all museums dwell on the past. Some are exhibit centers for the trends of today – recently created works of art, the ever-changing face of the digital world, and the emerging cultures that surround modern-day living. There is hardly a subject that does not take center stage at a museum somewhere in the United States or another part of the world.

Used to educate, inspire, enlighten, and inform, museums tell a story, and the people who work there are responsible for making that story accessible, engaging, captivating, and exciting. A well-crafted museum is the work of a carefully chosen team. Each member of the team is highly trained in an area of archival expertise that gives the museum an air of individuality that makes it stand out as a place to visit for a one-of-a-kind experience.

From the front entrance to the main exhibit hall to the gift shop, that special ambiance has to be there every step of the way in a museum. It can be quite a challenge for a museum director, curator, exhibit designer, archivist, conservator, registrar, collections manager, researcher, and the support staff working with them to keep exhibits fresh and relevant. These dedicated employees make the museum a hub of community activity, a place where something remarkable is always going on, an attraction that brings in visitors from far and wide, and has those living close by coming back time and again to see new exhibits or view the latest addition to an already vibrant collection.

This is a job where you can leave your mark, a career where discovery is encouraged. It provides you with a chance to go out and track down an artifact that will enhance the museum's collection and get people talking about a rare find, another piece of the puzzle that will unlock a mystery hidden somewhere in the past.

Museums are where people go to satisfy their curiosity because seeing is believing. They want to judge a piece of art for themselves, peruse an archaeological find, and – in those museums that allow it – touch an object that changed history. Those who visit a museum are seeking an unforgettable journey. Just imagine a career where you can help make that happen.

WHAT YOU CAN DO NOW

VOLUNTEERS ARE A VALUABLE resource for museums of all kinds and sizes. Volunteering at one of these institutions is an excellent way to find out if working in a museum is something you would enjoy doing.

Since all departments in a museum can use an extra hand, volunteers can usually be placed in most departments, from assisting the curator, to helping the conservator, to aiding archivists. You can even rotate among different departments to see which job you are most interested in.

Volunteers at museums usually have the flexibility of choosing how many hours a day or week they want to help out and which days they want to come in. It is a relaxed atmosphere in which to start learning about your future career.

If you live in an area where there are several museums, you might want to volunteer at more than one to get an idea of how the programs vary at the different locations. Take the time to research all different types of museums, and start determining which ones would appeal to you as the ideal workplace. There are museums that are geared toward adults, some that cater to children, and others that attract specific types of visitors, like sports fans, history buffs, or art connoisseurs.

While doing this research, also find out how large the staffs are at these facilities. This will give you a good idea of the job opportunities.

HISTORY OF THE CAREER

IN 15TH-CENTURY EUROPE, ITALIAN statesman Lorenzo de' Medici of Florence, was considered the consummate collector. Known as a patron of the arts, de' Medici (1449-1492) lived during the early part of the Renaissance period, which was a good time to be a collector. His collection encompassed all sorts of antiquities, including paintings, books, coins, and vases.

The de' Medici collection was so massive the term "museum" was used to describe it. At the time, that word was used to denote the comprehensiveness of a collection, not the building it was in. The collection could be viewed by friends and family members of de' Medici, but it was not open to the public. Though the collection was overwhelming, de' Medici kept a record of what he had and where he got it, making him a forerunner to the modern-day curator, archivist, or registrar.

By the 17th century, the term museum was widely used throughout Europe to describe large collections of curiosities. Danish physician

Olaus Wormius, known to the locals as Ole Worm, amassed one of those collections in Copenhagen. His collection included natural specimens, such as rocks, minerals, dried plants, and fossils. He had taxidermists stuff animals that once roamed the land around Copenhagen, and he kept those in his collection as well. Engravings were another passion of Ole Worm. He also kept accurate records of everything he had in his collection; in fact, a book was published cataloging his collectibles.

Upon his death in 1654, many of the physician's curiosities passed to another great collector, the Danish king, Frederick III, and it became part of the Royal Kunstkammer, or Cabinet of Curiosities. Still, these collections were not easily accessible to the general public.

That changed in 1683 in England, when Oxford University became the home of a unique collection. The collection was originally put together from the mid-1500s to the mid-1600s by John Tradescant and his son, also named John.

Both men were adventurers, horticulturalists, and world travelers. They brought back odd souvenirs from their worldwide travels, including exotic plants, rare minerals, and other finds. They built a large collection in their home in Lambeth, England. Father and son worked as curators of the assembled keepsakes.

The artifacts were acquired by noted wealthy British collector Elias Ashmole in 1664. He, in turn, presented the collection, along with many of his own antiquities, to Oxford University in 1677. There was a proviso attached to the gift, however; a building had to be constructed to house the collection and the public must be able to view all the relics.

When the building opened in 1683, it was referred to as a museum, the first use of the word to denote the building where these collections were put on display. The Ashmolean Museum is still today a highlight of the Oxford campus, and the entire collection is online at http://www.ashmolean.org

Two great European museums were established in the 18th century – the British Museum in London in 1759 and the Louvre in Paris in 1793. Both museums were enormous, and cataloging what they had in their collections, as well as caring for those items, was a tremendous task for the museum staff.

The importance of collecting artifacts of the time was not lost on the colonists in America. Many believed they were helping to develop a new land and felt the items used to make that happen should be preserved and handed down to future generations.

Most of the collecting was done informally, but in 1773, the Charleston (South Carolina) Library Society founded the Charleston Museum. Regarded as America's first museum, its mission was to record the history and maintain noteworthy artifacts of Charleston and the South Carolina coastal region.

The United States received one of its greatest gifts ever in 1829, when James Smithson left his half-million-dollar estate to the nation. The gift had to be used to establish the Smithsonian Institute in Washington DC, with the purpose of increasing and spreading knowledge.

The US Congress eventually established the institute in 1846 and it has grown to become the largest museum in the world. It is renowned not only for its collection, but for its knowledgeable and highly trained staff of curators, exhibit designers, conservators, researchers, registrars, archivists, and administrators. They have set the standard for how museums are operated.

In 1869, the American Museum of Natural History opened in New York City. It has become one of the preeminent scientific and cultural repositories in the world.

Shortly thereafter, a museum boom started in the United States. Museums were built all over the country during the late 1800s and into the early 1900s, and the period became known as the "Museum Age." Some of the more notable museums opened during that era were the Museum of Fine Arts in Boston (1870), the Metropolitan Museum of Art in New York City (1872), the Art Institute of Chicago (1879), the Portland Art Museum in Oregon (1892), the Field Museum of Natural History in Chicago (1893), and the Philadelphia Museum of Art (1925).

WHERE YOU WILL WORK

THERE ARE APPROXIMATELY 17,500 museums in the United States alone and more opening all the time, according to the American Alliance of Museums. The wide array of museums varies in size and the topics they cover. Some are located in bustling metropolitan areas, like New York City, Chicago, Los Angeles, or Dallas. Others are found in rural areas, small towns, or the suburbs.

The main difference from one museum to another is the focus or theme. People who are passionate about a particular subject, like American colonial history or World War II, can work at a facility that has those subjects as its theme. History museums may be very specific, covering the life of one individual, like George Washington (Mount Vernon, Virginia). They may also range more widely to offer a historical overview of an entire city, like Chicago (Chicago History Museum), or an in-depth look at the nation's past (National Museum of American History, Washington). They may cover one particular event – the Holocaust Museum in Washington and the National WWII Museum in New Orleans are examples.

Living history museums thrust visitors into a different time and place as they study what day-to-day life was like long before modern-day conveniences. Museum employees may be dressed in period garb, and visitors are surrounded by the sights and sounds of the past. Virginia's Colonial Williamsburg has long been recognized as one of the nation's outstanding living history museums.

Science and technology museums focus on important discoveries in biology, chemistry, physics, medicine, botany, ecology, and other disciplines. At the Museum of Science and Industry in Chicago, visitors can watch storm systems brewing at the Earth Revealed exhibit, among an array of other natural occurrences. In recent years, many science and technology museums have put an emphasis on getting visitors involved in hands-on activities so they can experience the wonders of the world of science for themselves. Natural history museums are where fossils, mammalogy, geology, mineralogy, astronomy, anthropology, and many other natural sciences take center stage.

Art museums are responsible for bringing works of outstanding aesthetic beauty to public view. Many people would have no other way of seeing the creations of some of the world's finest artists and sculptors – past and present – if not for the treasures displayed by these museums.

Sports museums house the artifacts of great athletes and the games they excelled in. The National Baseball Hall of Fame and Museum in Cooperstown, New York and the Pro Football Hall of Fame in Canton, Ohio are very popular destinations.

Children's museums emphasize learning through interaction. Unlike most museums, where exhibits are off-limits, these displays are designed for children to plunge right in and try things out for themselves.

THE WORK YOU WILL DO

MUSEUMS ARE KNOWN FOR THEIR serene, tranquil atmosphere, as visitors stroll through these great public spaces, taking in all the exhibits. Do not be fooled by that calm veneer – there is constant activity going on behind the scenes. Creating exhibits that bring visitors through the doors, adding to and maintaining collections, and keeping displays fresh and vibrant, are some of the activities of the museum staff.

Museum Director

Every team needs a leader, and in museums that person is the director. A director is usually a seasoned professional who comes to the museum after years in the field, with a complete understanding of every aspect of running an institution.

The director coordinates all the activity that is going on at the museum, and guides the staff, while taking their insight and advice into consideration. Working with the museum's board of directors, the museum director sets policy and is responsible for the financial health of the institution. Since most museums are nonprofit operations, fundraising plays a key role in keeping a museum financially solvent. Coming up with creative ways of running yearly fundraising campaigns – getting the public to support the museum – is an essential part of the director's job.

The director has input into what the museum adds to its collection, as well as what exhibits and special events will be brought in. One of the most important roles of any director is being the public face of the museum – the person who represents the institution in the community and media.

Curator

The person who knows the most about a museum's collections is the curator. The curator comes to the position with an extensive background in the subject covered by the museum. Large museums, like the Museum of Fine Arts in Boston, have a staff of curators, with one member serving as the head curator. Curators know every piece the museum has in its collection, whether it is currently on display or not, and what significance it has in history. They know how and where the piece fits into the institution's collection, and the way it should be displayed.

When it comes to adding new items and objects to the museum's collection, the curator determines what is needed and directs the search for the object. The curator must determine the authenticity of each piece before acquiring it for the museum's collection. This is done by seeking out documentation for the object in question as well as its provenance. Curators make sure a museum's collection has a semblance of order, an organized flow and focus, and is not just a hodgepodge of collectibles.

Conservator

While curators are knowledgeable about how to store and care for a collection, the bulk of that job falls to expertly trained conservators. The work of a conservator is crucial to slowing, if not stopping, the decaying process.

There are many factors to consider when preserving historic items. Over time, fiber, paper, ceramics, wood, paintings, textiles, bones, metals, and other materials deteriorate in different ways and under a variety of conditions. Being able to exhibit items with the proper casing or framing, heat and humidity, and lighting, so as not to cause damage to the object requires study and expertise.

Every museum has many more items in its collection than it displays, and often rotates items on display throughout the year. Proper storage of each item, to meet its individual needs while it is not on display, is essential. The conservator oversees that storage process, in addition to making sure the object is cleaned properly before storage and while it is on display. Conservators also restore objects, making repairs when needed or replacing missing pieces if the object is received in an incomplete condition.

Registrar

The registrar keeps track of every item in the museum's collection. The registrar is in charge of making sure all the information about an object is correct and up-to-date. That includes the date the museum acquired a particular object, how it was obtained, the cost, and any other relevant information.

Categorizing and numbering items are duties of the registrar. If a museum lends some of its items out to another archival institution, the registrar handles all the paperwork for the transaction. Making arrangements for having the items packed properly, shipped, and insured, and arranging all the permissions necessary to secure the loan are the responsibility of the registrar. Some museums refer to the position as the collections manager.

Archivist

The archivist keeps an accurate history of all objects in a museum's collection. If an item came with a letter, a bill of sale, photographs, newspaper articles about it, or was written about in a personal diary that was included with the object, it all gets filed and becomes a permanent part of the archival collection. If any research is done on the object, that gets filed as well. The archivist keeps accurate records of anything related to exhibits the museum brings in or special events.

Exhibit Designer

People go to museums to view exhibits, which is why the work of exhibit designers is so important. There may be one chief designer on staff to handle day-to-day work, with more exhibit designers brought in for new exhibits and special projects. Large museums usually have a full-time staff of several designers. Exhibit designers work with curators to develop ideas for permanent and temporary displays.

While exhibits were once designed solely to be looked at, that is no longer the case. Today's exhibits can often be walked on, touched, and played with, and include knobs that can be turned, buttons that can be pushed, and objects that can be moved around. Museum visitors want to be involved in the exhibit and try it out. This hands-on approach gives designers an array of challenges.

Working with drawings, scale models, computers, video screens, animatronics, acoustics, and lighting, exhibit designers make each display in a museum look different, contain something special, and, if possible, include something totally unexpected. It all has to be done within a budget and be completed by a specified deadline.

Many exhibits include a computer or other technical components, so having a technology specialist on staff is useful. Not only is this specialist needed to troubleshoot equipment should a problem arise, but the museum also has to have someone to install the equipment properly when the exhibit is first installed.

Researcher

In a history museum, a researcher might be asked to track down information about an object, and find out as much as possible about the period in which the item was made, and the kind of people who might have used it, like ranchers or farmers, or city dwellers. In art museums, researchers may be asked to look into when and where a particular piece was created, and its place in the artist's work.

Some researchers have a writing background and write the text for labels and signs that go next to objects when on display. Large museums often publish a catalog to go along with a major exhibit, and researchers put together the information contained in that reference guide. New pieces are coming into museums all the time, and while the staff may know something about the object, the researcher develops a complete history.

Education Director

Education directors are playing a more important role in museums. Schools are encouraged to use nearby museums to help bring classroom lessons to life. Classes and workshops are held about various aspects of the museum's collection to help people of all ages gain a greater appreciation for all the items on display. Informative tours, with time taken to discuss particular exhibits in detail, are offered to visitors who want to study the museum's collection in greater depth. Those tours are put together and hosted by the museum's education director. Museums are expanding their educational base with outreach programs and special events developed by education directors.

Oral Historian

In recent years, museums have taken the opportunity to record history in the actual voices of the people who lived through it. This is the job of the oral historian. The recordings can be done in audio and video. The usual format is question and answer, with the interview conducted by the oral historian based on background assembled by the museum researcher. These accounts in the words of the people who lived through the events would be lost forever if not preserved by the oral historian.

Living History Museums

Living history museums, like Colonial Williamsburg in Virginia, are set in another period and everything has to be as realistic as possible in order to transport visitors back in time. All museum employees who come in contact with visitors are dressed in period costumes, so living history museums employ a *costumer.* Much like a costume designer in the movies, the costumer makes sure museum employees are outfitted in authentic period seasonal dress.

Most living history museums require that costumes be authentic to the period, right down to the undergarments. Costumers have to be familiar with the fabrics of the period, the styles and colors of the time, for both men and women.

Some of the costumed staff lead tours and give talks, and they have to speak the way people did during the period represented. They also have to answer questions the way someone would have who lived during that time. The people who fill these jobs are called *character interpreters,* and they are usually actors. They are trained for their roles and directed by the head character interpreter, who comes to the job with an in-depth knowledge of the history and time period.

MUSEUM PROFESSIONALS TELL THEIR STORIES

I Am a Museum Exhibit Designer

"This is an exciting time to be in this career. There is just so much going on when it comes to exhibit design. The expansion of children's museums with their hands-on exhibits, the use of computers, and the latest technology makes this an ever-changing, fast-paced facet of museum work.

Today, you are encouraged to push the envelope in exhibit design. I feel free to be creative and come up with new ideas. There is really nothing that's impossible in design work today, if you have the financial backing. Some of these ideas for exhibit design are so groundbreaking and innovative that many corporations are willing to fund a project in a museum just to be associated with a cutting-edge design concept that everybody is talking about and will be trying to copy.

I think the field is competitive, and that makes it fun and challenging. A part of you wants to see what someone else has come up with and then you want to see if you can go one better. The people who benefit love to go to museums and see something fresh and pioneering.

It all starts with an idea – brainstorming sessions with curators, researchers, the museum director, and members of the design staff. Sometimes it comes down to finding a way to breathe new life into an exhibit that has been in the museum for a while and needs updating.

Most of the work I do is presenting an exhibit being brought into the museum for anywhere from a few months to a year. As an exhibit designer, you must have a feel for each exhibit, and understand what you need to do so visitors will get the most enjoyment when they come to see it. It's about what you can do to bring someone right into that exhibit, to feel part of it, to see the exhibit from all angles.

You start with drawings, sketching out several different ideas. We use the same exhibit space for all traveling exhibits, so when one leaves I want to make absolutely sure that the next exhibit coming in looks nothing like the last one. Some of it has to do with the artifacts in the exhibit, but it also depends on the presentation.

Once drawings are completed we might make models of certain aspects of the exhibit to show how it will look. Once all ideas are approved, we start building the exhibit. You have to know the audience an exhibit is geared to. With kids you want to have all the bells and whistles, the latest colors, lights, and sounds. With an older crowd, you want them to feel comfortable with an exhibit. You don't want to include technology they don't know much about. At the same time, you do want to wow them a bit.

What's great about working in a museum is that an exhibit is here long enough for me to visit it when the museum is closed, tweak it a bit, and give myself a critique. You learn from every exhibit you do and I hope I never stop wanting to make the next design even better."

I Am a Researcher at a Living History Museum

"I have been a researcher at several different types of museums, and working at a living history museum is by far the most exciting. At a living history museum, researchers play a vital role in making the museum a trip back in time.

While my job title at all the museums I've worked at has always been researcher, I've viewed my job as being a historical detective, and that is certainly true at a living history museum. At this museum everything has to be authentic to the time period represented here. People who come to this museum really know their history and they expect everything to be perfect. So if someone should challenge some detail at the museum, no matter how small or insignificant, we have to be ready to document that what is presented is totally accurate. That means verifying everything we do with a number of highly respected sources.

Research is used in museums in various ways. People always want to donate what they believe is a rare or valuable object to a museum. It might be a family heirloom that comes with a story, which has been handed down through the years, but that's about it when it comes to documentation.

Naturally, museums can't take everything that's offered, but if there is an object that the museum is interested in, and there is some question about authenticity, how it was used, if it has been modified in any way, what it is made of, where it was made, and a host of other issues, a researcher will be brought in on the case. You check out the object from all different angles and, if there was a manufacturer involved in making it, you try to unearth all you can about that company. It's a matter of following leads.

When it comes to the history of an object, researchers go through all types of written material, including letters, diaries, and personal accounts. In addition, film, photographs, and drawings are thoroughly searched to get as much precise information as possible.

Researchers are also assigned to track down all the pertinent data needed to make an exhibit look as realistic as possible. At a living history museum, researchers work to get the exact details needed to make the restoration of a historical room or building as precise as possible. They work with costumers to research attire worn by character interpreters. They may also do research on the characters themselves so all portrayals are accurate."

I Am a Curator at a Mid-Sized Natural History Museum

"I came to this job after serving as a curator at a much smaller natural history museum. At that museum I also served as director, something curators often do at smaller institutions. As the curator/director I was in charge of the museum's staff, and I made all the administrative decisions. I also spent a great deal of time on fundraising. That was in addition to being responsible for the museum's entire collection.

Here at this museum I don't have those additional duties, since I only serve as the curator, and that frees me up to focus full time on the collection. The curator's job in itself is quite a handful. Curators have to know everything there is to know about a museum's collection. You must have a complete understanding of the world these objects came from and convey that through the way the items are exhibited.

Most museums have many more pieces than can be displayed at one time. Some items are always on display because they are a draw. These are items in our collection that the museum is known for and built its reputation on. It's what brings people through the door. Other objects are put on display only during certain times of the year and are replaced by different items on a rotating basis. I think this attracts people during different seasons. It always gives visitors something different to see and has them coming back to the museum more than once a year.

Items are removed from display for a short period of time so they can be cleaned. Caring for items is very important. Caring for an item only takes a day or two, and then it's back on display.

Everything that goes on in a museum is a team effort. When it comes to setting up a new exhibit, I meet with the exhibit designer and we kick around ideas. Figuring it all out is like a puzzle, and the pieces have to come together.

I also help bring in special exhibits to the museum that I find out are available and that I feel will draw a crowd, get us some publicity, and cause some excitement. I work with our exhibit designer so we can make these traveling displays something special when they are here in our building.

Acquisitions are something else that a curator does, usually with input from the museum director. Most museums do not have a huge acquisition budget, so we try to get rare objects donated, but sometimes you just need to add something to the collection and purchasing it is the only way to get it. We try to have a mix of items that are specific to the local area, as well as items that you will not see around these parts. The right mix of objects is important, as a museum is a mix – of learning, enlightenment, and entertainment. We want people to have a good time when they come here and always find out something they didn't know before they got here."

PERSONAL QUALIFICATIONS

MUSEUM PROFESSIONALS HAVE many traits in common that help them succeed in their careers, and topping the list is excellent communications skills. Curators, conservators, exhibit designers, museum directors, researchers, and technology specialists work together on a series of projects and must be able to communicate their ideas clearly and succinctly to each other. Whether you are speaking at a staff meeting, or putting your thoughts down in writing, the way you present information to coworkers helps set a tone, chart a course, motivate, and instill confidence in your work.

Strong writing skills help museum professionals throughout their careers. Preparing grant applications, labeling exhibits, developing educational materials, promoting the museum, recording information about an exhibit or objects in a collection, writing reports, or collaborating on a scholarly article, are just a few of the many ways a good command of the written word will help you in your work.

Museums are a people-oriented business. Whether working with other staff members or museum visitors, interpersonal skills are a must. Respecting other workers and volunteers, making them feel appreciated for all they do, recognizing the role they play in making the museum a success – all are vital to the morale of the staff. A staff that is valued tends to pass on that good feeling to museum visitors, making them feel welcome, and creating a friendly atmosphere that encourages people to return and recommend that their friends and neighbors visit.

There are always many things going on at a museum, and there will hardly be a day during your career that you will not find yourself multitasking. Doing more than one thing at a time has to be second nature to you in this job.

With a limited budget or a deadline looming, you might find that you do not have everything you need to complete a project exactly the way you want, especially in the time frame you have been given. You have to be resourceful, realizing there is more than one way to get things accomplished and knowing how to make do.

When you work in a museum the words "can't do" are not in your vocabulary. That means you have to be flexible and creative in order to make the impossible happen. Your creativity will be called upon time and again.

Creativity goes hand and hand with imagination. These traits, together with an unending curiosity, allow people working in the museum field to raise the bar on every project.

To succeed in museum work, you must have a passion for making exhibits at the museum exciting not only for the visitors who come to see them but also for the staff members who put these unique displays together. The commitment of the staff comes through in everything that goes on at the museum. There is a mission, everyone understands what it is, and the staff works together to accomplish it.

ATTRACTIVE FEATURES

WHETHER FOR A GROUP OF WIDE-EYED youngsters looking at something they thought was simply not possible until they saw it demonstrated at the museum, or a couple of senior citizens reminiscing about their youth after seeing an item from that era on display in an exhibit, the world surrounding archival wonders is stimulating and invigorating. It turns an ordinary day into an adventure for museum visitors, and your efforts make that experience possible. There are not many careers where you can leave your office for a few minutes each day and watch people enjoy the direct results of your work.

Museum work is very fulfilling. Each time you help put together a successful exhibit, you derive a great sense of accomplishment. This is a career where you are bringing art and culture into the community. It is uplifting for everyone who comes to the museum to see the artifacts contained in it.

Part of your job is to enlighten and educate the public, so you create a greater understanding of the items in the museum. You are on an exciting mission to help the museum grow, to expand its collection, to get more people interested in the important work that is going on at the institution. Together with the rest of the museum staff, you set goals, see them reached, and witness the impact that success has on the museum itself and the cultural life of the community.

Working in a museum, you are surrounded by creative people all the time, exchanging ideas on a daily basis. Developing exhibits from the very early stages until completion is a mainstay of this profession. You are there at the beginning and follow a project every step of way, tweaking it as it goes along to make sure it comes out exactly right. This is hands-on work, where every member of the team makes an important contribution.

Museums offer a very exciting work environment. All you need to do to get some inspiration is take a walk through the exhibit halls. Who else has the time to explore all the items on display in a museum and has a chance to think of ways to expand the exhibits and infuse even more energy into them?

In this career, you are surrounded by a subject you love. You are free to follow your passion and you are paid for doing it. Artifacts proudly displayed in exhibits throughout the museum often document your successes and your years of hard work.

This is a field where you never stop learning and always remain on the hunt for that next great find. Exchanging information with colleagues in the museum field is encouraged. That gives you an opportunity to share some of the knowledge you have gained through the years, as you dig deeper into your field of expertise.

UNATTRACTIVE ASPECTS

MOST MUSEUMS GO THROUGH BUDGET crunches from time to time, and that limits the acquisitions, programs, and even the staff at these facilities. For those working at the museum, this can be very frustrating, especially when you know there are ways to improve exhibits, refurbish the building, and provide more services to patrons, but there simply is not enough money in the budget to get it done.

Some museums have to battle budget problems on an annual basis, and many members of the staff have to take on fundraising responsibilities. Not everyone is comfortable asking for contributions, and many people feel it takes them away from the work they should be doing. In order to accomplish what they want, such as the restoration of an artifact, they might have to launch a fundraising drive and wait until the money comes in before the project can get started.

Fundraising efforts often take longer than expected and project delays are commonplace, but nonetheless exasperating. So patience is truly a virtue in this job, in addition to an upbeat attitude with a focus on how great the project will be once it is completed. If you are impatient about getting things done this could be a frustrating work environment.

Tight budgets also mean that museum personnel might have to take on more than one job in order to help the museum thrive. Doing more than one job in a museum rarely means getting more than one salary or even a raise. However, that is how museums survive during tough financial times.

Museum work is detailed, painstaking, and time-consuming. You could be working on a particular project for some time. If a quick turnaround and getting onto something new is your style, museum work might not be for you. Many museum jobs, including conservator, archivist, curator, and registrar, involve very exacting and time- consuming work.

Your work is usually behind the scenes. People who are part of a museum staff rarely see their names in the headlines. That means you generally work in anonymity, getting little public acclaim. All the credit for a job well done is going to go to the staff as a whole and to the museum. Your colleagues will recognize your hard work, and you will be able to take personal pride in it, but the public at large will rarely see or know about everything you did to make a project successful.

EDUCATION AND TRAINING

THERE ARE SEVERAL DIFFERENT educational paths you could take in preparing for a career in museum work. Many museum professionals earn a degree in an academic discipline, such as archaeology, geology, genealogy, astronomy, history, fine art, art history, or a related topic. This is especially true of curators, who must have an in-depth knowledge of the particular field in which the museum specializes. Curators usually possess at least a master's degree, and many go on to earn a PhD.

Because students majoring in certain academic fields are preparing for careers in museum work, some colleges are now offering courses in museum studies as a minor. Florida State University, for example, through its Art History Department, has an undergraduate minor in museum studies, which includes an internship.

The University of Michigan offers an undergraduate minor in museum studies with courses such as Museums and Society, and Contemporary Issues in Museums.

Other colleges that have minors in museum studies include the University of Texas at El Paso, College at Brockport (New York), Lynchburg College in Virginia, and University of Wyoming in Laramie. This is a very popular subject and it is a rapidly growing minor at colleges all over the nation.

Many colleges are developing certificate programs in museum studies at the graduate level. Students can enroll in these programs while pursuing a graduate-level degree in another discipline or after completing work on a graduate degree. Some of the colleges that make these certificate programs available are Northern Illinois University, University of Wisconsin–Milwaukee, Columbian College of Arts & Sciences in Washington DC, and California State University–Long Beach. Many of these museum studies certificate programs require a short internship.

Programs for these graduate certificates in museum studies are becoming more commonplace as those who excel in a particular academic field seek to parlay that into a museum career. Students can take either the museum studies minor on the undergraduate level, the graduate museum studies certificate program, or both, in conjunction with their other studies, to gain training and credentials in the museum field.

Technology specialists who want to go into museum work would combine their computer science major with a museum studies minor. Costumers who get a Bachelor of Fine Arts degree with an emphasis on fashion and design, and have an eye toward working in a living history museum, might take a minor in museum studies. Oral historians would get a master's degree in a specialized area of history and add some museum science courses. Education directors often come to museums with a teaching background, but sometimes have a degree in an academic discipline specific to the museum, and augment that with some courses in elementary education, secondary education, or a museum science certificate.

Library science is the course of study for those looking for careers as archivists, researchers, registrars, and collection managers. The University of Nebraska–Omaha has three different undergraduate programs in library science, and the University of Southern Mississippi offers a BA in library science and information.

Most museums want to hire archivists, researchers, registrars, and collection managers with a master's degree in library science. There are many colleges throughout the nation where you can earn a graduate degree in library science, including the University of Illinois at Urbana-Champaign, University of Maryland at College Park, University of North Carolina at Chapel Hill, and University of Pittsburgh.

While many museum directors come from the ranks of curators, some do complete museum studies programs. Other museum administrators who work in the business offices at large museums throughout the country also approach the job with a degree in museum studies.

One of the foremost museum studies programs in the United States can be found at Tusculum College in Greenville, Tennessee. In addition to its extensive array of museum-related courses, this museum studies program operates two archival institutions on campus. The Doak House Museum is the home of the school's co-founder, and the other is the President Andrew Johnson Museum and Library. Most students graduating with a bachelor's degree in museum studies from Tusculum College have spent substantial time gaining valuable experience at one of the two museums.

Exhibit designers get their training in graphic, industrial, or commercial design. They attend schools like Pratt Institute or Parsons, The New School for Design in New York City, or the California College of the Arts in San Francisco/Oakland. Some attend universities that have a graphic arts program, like the Stamps School of Art & Design at the University of Michigan.

Conservators may pursue undergraduate degrees in a variety of subjects, including chemistry, art history, anthropology, and archaeology. It is the graduate work that really prepares you to be a conservator. Anyone going into this field has to be handy; good in the sciences, especially chemistry; and have a passion for preserving items. Colleges with highly recognized programs for degrees for conservators include Columbia University in New York City, University of Delaware in Newark, New York University in New York City, and Buffalo (New York) State College.

EARNINGS

THE BEST-PAYING JOBS IN THE museum field are usually found at the largest institutions. Some of the highest salaries are earned at museums like the Smithsonian Institute, which has 6,300 employees in total – almost 300 of them curators. Museum of Natural History in New York City, Philadelphia Museum of Art, Museum of Fine Arts in Boston, and other well-established institutions also pay well.

Museum professionals usually have to work their way up to jobs at these renowned institutions. That means starting out at small museums.

Besides the size of a museum, another consideration when it comes to salary is education. If you have a master's degree, you will not earn as high a salary as someone with a doctorate. Experience is also factored in. That is why people in this field often work at smaller museums while studying for a graduate degree. That way they are gaining experience while completing their education.

This is a field where patience and perseverance do eventually pay off, though most museum professionals admit that they do not enter the field for the money. Curators with a master's degree begin their careers earning in the $35,000 range, but can end up making a salary of $100,000 after they get a PhD and some experience.

Museum directors start out with a salary of roughly $40,000 at a small museum and can earn between $125,000 and $175,000 at a large museum in a major city.

Conservators and exhibit designers have entry-level salaries of about $35,000 a year, but both can earn upwards of $65,000. In large museums, where a conservator or exhibit designer can head up a department, that salary may increase to $80,000.

Registrars, collection managers, archivists, researchers, oral historians, costumers, and education directors find their salary range begins around $25,000 and can go as high as $65,000. Technology specialists start their careers in the $30,000 range, and department directors can earn $80,000 annually.

Character interpreters are usually paid an hourly rate, but the department head makes between $30,000 and $40,000 a year.

OPPORTUNITIES

MORE THAN 400,000 PEOPLE ARE employed by museums throughout the United States, according to the American Alliance of Museums (AAM). That number continues to grow as more museums open all the time.

Americans love museums, and that means expanding career opportunities. The AAM reports that an average of 850 million people visit museums in the United States every year. That is more than the combined number of people who visit theme parks and attend major league sporting events annually!

Experts in the field predict that the number of jobs at museums – including directors, curators, conservators, exhibit designers, and archivists – will grow over 15 percent during the next decade.

In addition, museums have proved to be good for the economy in the communities where they are located. They help bring in tourists, who spend money in nearby hotels, restaurants, theaters, and stores. It is estimated that museums contribute over $20 billion annually to the nation's economy. That means communities want to help local museums grow so they can continue to attract visitors.

Developing a career in museums is about getting experience. Not everyone who wants to be a curator starts out in that job. Many people take on other positions, like registrar, archivist, or researcher as they wait for their big break. Having hands-on experience in other areas of museum work helps increase your value, since you have insight into all aspects of the field.

Museums operate in a very competitive world. People who work at these institutions are always searching for innovative and imaginative ways of presenting to the public the art and artifacts they collect. Museums are always looking for people with original ideas. People who have a solid portfolio of work at either another museum they have worked for or a related business, like an art gallery or an auction house, will receive positive attention when looking for new opportunities.

GETTING STARTED

BECAUSE THERE IS SUCH AN EMPHASIS on experience, internships are an excellent way to get started. Many college programs that award a degree in museum studies require an internship. These internships are rather intensive, and the practical experience gained through these programs is considered a vital first step.

This is one field where experience, including volunteer work, is valued and weighs heavily during the job-seeking process and job interviews. The more wide-ranging the experience, the better. Those pursuing a career in the world of museums work their way up the ladder, so starting out in an entry-level position is the norm.

Museum and museum associations are very helpful in working with people who want to find a career. Full- and part-time positions are usually posted on museum websites and are easily accessible. In addition, organizations for museum professionals, like the American Alliance of Museums (AAM) have online job sites.

Regional museum associations with job sites include Western Museums Association, Southeastern Museums Conference, Association of Midwest Museums, New England Museum Association, Mid-Atlantic Association of Museums, and Mountain-Plains Museum Association. Not only are these job sites a good way to gauge what positions are available, but they also specify what various museums are looking for in their employees. Listed on these sites are a number of entry-level positions, as well as jobs for people who are more advanced in their careers.

Another good way to get started is to work with a mentor. People who have worked in museums for a long time have not forgotten what it was like to follow their passion and find their first job in a museum. Many are more than happy to work with students or even those who have already graduated from college, and pass along some of what they have learned during their years working at a museum.

People who work in museums are generally a close-knit group, who recognize the important role these institutions play in society, and who welcome new and dedicated people into the field. Networking – especially with the help of a mentor at first – can be very valuable as you embark on your museum career, and will serve you well throughout your years in the field.

REGIONAL ASSOCIATIONS

■ **Western Museums Association**
http://www.westmuse.org/job_board

■ **Southeastern Museums Conference**
http://www.semcdirect.net/job-listings

■ **Association of Midwest Museums**
www.midwestmuseums.org/jobs.html

■ **New England Museum Association**
http://www.nemanet.org/resources/career-center/nema-jobs

■ **Mid-Atlantic Association of Museums**
www.midatlanticmuseums.org/news-for-the-field/jobs
-in-the-region.html

■ **Mountain-Plains Museum Association**
http://www.mpma.net/jobs.php

NATIONAL ASSOCIATIONS

■ **American Alliance of Museums (AAM)**
http://www.aam-us.org

■ **Small Museum Association (SMA)**
http://www.smallmuseum.org

■ **The Association for Living History, Farm and Agricultural Museums** http://www.alhfam.org

■ **Association of African American Museums (AAAM)**
http://www.blackmuseums.org/about/history.htm

■ **The Association of Art Museum Curators (AAMC)**
http://www.artcurators.org

■ **Association of Art Museum Directors**
https://aamd.org

■ **Association of Science-Technology Centers (ASTC)**
http://www.astc.org/about/index.htm

■ **National Association for Museum Exhibition (NAME)**
http://name-aam.org/home

■ **Association of Children's Museums**
http://www.childrensmuseums.org

■ **Association of Academic Museums & Galleries (AAMG)**
http://www.aamg-us.org/index.php

WEBSITES

■ **International Association of Curators of Contemporary Art**
http://www.iktsite.org

■ **Independent Curators International**
http://curatorsintl.org

■ **International Council of Museums**
http://icom.museum

■ **Museums Journal**
http://www.museumsassociation.org
/museums-journal

■ **Society of American Archivists (SAA)**
http://www2.archivists.org

SCHOOL WEBSITES

■ **Florida State University**
http://arthistory.fsu.edu/Undergraduate/Programs/Minors

■ **The University of Michigan**
www.lsa.umich.edu/histart/undergraduate/museumstudiesmin
or

■ **University of Texas at El Paso**
http://academics.utep.edu/Default.aspx?tabid=66365

■ **College at Brockport (New York)**
www.brockport.edu/history/museum_studies.html

■ **Lynchburg College (Virginia)**
https://www.lynchburg.edu/museum-studies-minor

■ **University of Wyoming**
http://www.uwyo.edu/museumstudies

■ **Northern Illinois University**
http://www.niu.edu/mstudies

■ **University of Wisconsin–Milwaukee**
http://www4.uwm.edu/letsci/museumstudies

■ **Columbian College of Arts & Sciences (Washington DC)**
http://museumstudies.columbian.gwu.edu/museum
-studies-graduate-certificate-program

■ **California State University–Long Beach**
www.csulb.edu/divisions/aa/catalog/current/cota/art/art_ct02
.html

■ **University of Nebraska–Omaha**
http://www.unomaha.edu/libraryed/undergrad

■ **University of Southern Mississippi**
www.usm.edu/undergraduate/library-and-information-science
-ba

■ **University of Maryland at College Park**
http://ischool.umd.edu

■ **University of North Carolina at Chapel Hill**
https://sils.unc.edu

■ **University of Pittsburgh**
http://www.ischool.pitt.edu/lis

■ **Tusculum College**
http://www2.tusculum.edu
/museumstudiesprogram

■ **Parsons, The New School for Design**
http://www.newschool.edu/parsons

■ **California College of the Arts**
https://www.cca.edu/academics/graphic-design

■ **Stamps School of Art & Design at the University of Michigan**
http://www.art-design.umich.edu

■ **Columbia University**
http://www.arch.columbia.edu/programs/historic-preservation

■ **University of Delaware in Newark**
http://www.artcons.udel.edu/undergraduate

■ **New York University**
http://www.nyu.edu/gsas/dept/fineart/conservation/index.ht

■ **Buffalo State College**
http://artconservation.buffalostate.edu

Website www.careers-internet.org

For information on other Careers Reports please contact

service@careers-internet.org

www.ingramcontent.com/pod-product-compliance
Lightning Source LLC
Chambersburg PA
CBHW070755180526
45168CB00004B/1626